Cairn

Marking the Trace

Cameron Miller

Unsolicited Press
Portland, Oregon
www.unsolicitedpress.com
orders@unsolicitedpress.com
619-354-8005

-

Cover Design: Kathryn Gerhardt
Editors: Analieze Cervantes; S.R. Stewart
ISBN: 978-1-950730-46-9

To winter coated mountains and birch, summer lakes and autumn skies, not to mention the god who speaks in the frozen creaks of trees, the jagged wind across bitter ice, from out of the whispered path of fallen stars, the soft darkness of solitude, and even amidst the loneliness of depression. These are poems arising from life in the Northeast Kingdom of Vermont and the Finger Lakes of New York. Thank you, wild and sacred beauty.

Contents

A Poem that Breathed Air

The first poem to be born and live was from a fortune cookie.

I never stopped walking in the garden of poetry after a course on T. S. Eliot in seminary. Still, after twenty-five years of harvesting poems every Sunday to replace the Apostle Paul and tie together the Hebrew Scripture and Gospel, I failed to write one that lived. No matter how inspired I felt by an event, emotion, vision, or person, every effort was awkward and wooden. Years and years of reading Mary Oliver, Billy Collins, Wendell Berry, Anne Sexton, Li-young Li, Marie Howe, Rabia of Basra, Kabir, Rumi, and Tagore did not equip me with the ability to write a poem I would allow to breathe the light of day.

Then, alone just before closing in a Chinese restaurant in Newport, Vermont, my cookie crumbled and at its center was a curled fortune. Immediately upon reading that fortune I wrote the rudiments of a poem on my used napkin and knew, deep down in my bones, it would live. What changed? Or was it simply the accumulation of all those poets whispering in my ear?

Living in the Northeast Kingdom of Vermont, surrounded by wild and rugged beauty softens the soul even as it hardens life. For decades before Vermont, I prided myself on being able to pick out the sacred in the twisted rust of urban life, perceiving beauty where others only saw neglect and the refuse of congested society. In prose and in preaching, I insisted that if the holy was indeed present in our midst then perceiving it in the tangle of concrete, steel, and the smudged ordinary had to be possible. I still think so.

Looking back from a distance now, it seems to me that the sheer quantity of human activity, angst, pain, and rubble crashing in waves of stimulation and intensity on my life in the city, began to eat away at my sensory awareness. Shades and filters formed to protect me from the profound "too much." Incrementally, without notice, cataracts formed to soften the blow of what splashed from all around. Over time, less and less penetrated the protective film. I did not notice until well grounded in the Northeast Kingdom with newly unclogged pores.

Perhaps it is possible to prevent such loss of perception, and blunt the diminishment of vision and hearing required of poetry and painting. But until I lived in Vermont, in a home of supreme quiet on a lake surrounded by lightly inhabited mountains, I had no clue that my sight had dulled or my hearing of the still small voice had weakened.

The sudden change broke the seal and peeled away the edges of the plastic wrap. I could hear so much more of the small and insignificant sounds when "loud" became honking geese. I found myself looking at everything. I would stop the car on the dusty shoulder of a poorly paved road and gawk at the texture of birch mingled with pine and mixed in with ash and poplar, and how the colors change from summer to winter canvass – both brilliant in their own right. Such arrested driving or walking was a daily occurrence.

The color of the lake changed month to month. I heard birds again – Chickadees and Crows all year long but with songs that changed by the season. A daily convention of geese met at night outside our window in autumn, and I re-learned the songs of Robbins, Finches, and Jays. Skunks and Fishers sniffed their way at dawn and a coterie of deer wandered the neighborhood at night.

The darkness spawned a rash of stars so vast and intense it mesmerized me even in sub-zero temperatures. Especially then, because the atmosphere between soil and heaven seemed to disappear in frigid air. Dog and I would stop and stare into the sky, standing motionless in the cold blackness knowing an unseen herd of deer pawed through snow a football toss away. In warm weather, I would lie on my back on the driveway with dog on alert at my side, feasting on the brilliant mystery receding upward.

It softened me and returned my mind to openness and receptivity amidst the awareness that a film had formed and was now dissolving. It was not merely passive though. I found myself aggressively listening to the world all around — vigorously watching the minute as well as the grand.

It was this hyper-active perceiving that gave birth to poems that lived. I yearned to share what I was knowing. I groaned with pleasure and wanted to give it. Could I hold a single moment in my hands and heart and paint it with words in such a way that a reader, whoever it might be, could step into it with me?

The prose and preaching continued, sometimes getting in the way. Often, they took up so much space and oxygen in the room that little was left for poems. But then my first novel, the ostensive reason I had retreated from full-time parish ministry, was complete and out in the world. I had time for poetry again.

The looking and listening had not stopped, and I was more gluttonous than ever to behold the immense abundance all around.

Moving to upstate New York, to the Finger Lakes region, was a shock to the system. Still beautiful, it lacked the wildness of the Northeast Kingdom. Even more, I lived in town. I landed in a leafy college town surrounded by the pastoral beauty of vineyards and farms on the shores of a glistening lake. Who could complain? But the canopy of stars was much thinner. The wildness was gone. The listening and the watching turned inward, wandering unaccompanied through the darkness of the mind – my mind.

Now there were essays to be written as well, a weekly newspaper column insisting on a deadline. The watching and listening turned outward to the more domesticated nature around me, the tree lined lawns and lanes, and an historic cemetery on my street. Now the oak I watched was older and gnarly, and it mingled with what I heard in dreams, and in conversations all around me. The inside and the outside intersected, and the strange back and forth demanded to be shared. Poetry, prose, and essay each insisted on their due, but they also shifted shapes and began to meld. I was not always sure when I opened my laptop, what form I was writing. Since the fortune cookie, the poet has longed to be dominant but never won in competition with the preacher, novelist, or essayist. Now, perhaps, that may be changing.

These poems and essays were seen and heard in the Northeast Kingdom and Finger Lakes. Their unknowing collaborators are the people I know and strangers I met. Mostly though, they were mined from the crystals and stalactites within the darkened shelter of my own mind in conversation with the world around me. The poems dance with the essays as different forms apprehending common themes. Sometimes they are graceful together, but awkward too. My hope is you find an open window or door here, one or more that you can crawl through.

Cameron Miller
Finger Lakes, New York
2020

MARKING THE TRACE

Poems of Nature, Human Nature, and the Sacred

NATURE

Finity

The kestrel, an imperial look
flung over her shoulder,
rains disapproval upon my interruption.
She is scornful of my presence, now paranoid
I might steal her breakfast
of beheaded mourning dove at my feet.
Dove quills and bits of tuft
splotch the sidewalk, the remnant plumage
and fuzzies separated from their host
an ugly pile of dawn litter.
I stare at the headless body with skin puckered
closed at the neck, a drawstring bag
of pale gray feathers.

Death's beady black eyes
thicken my blood to gravy.
My eyes dart from lifeless body
to feathered carnage
to motionless predator.

In the shadow of finity
hope circles the drain—inevitably,
invariably swallowed
by death's gravity
pulling us down into fatality.

How will I die?

Better to be guillotined like the dove
or scraped from the inside out by cancer?

What about rotting into the blood-black humus
beneath a remote clutter of trees,
maggots and beetles licking out my sinuses
the second or third setting after vultures
and opossums have carve away recognition?

Does method matter?

If some deaths are senseless
which ones are sensefull?
Will it matter at the moment
I become extinct – no one like me
left anywhere on the planet?

That kestrel is unmolested
by thoughts of death.

Wind on Snow

Wind blows tiny ghost horses
spinning in herds across white dunes
left
  then right, zig
then zag
disappearing over a mound
never reaching the lake
beneath two feet of snow
on four feet of ice.
I see it all

from my window.

Eleven Below in Vermont

Onyx dome over pastures of snow
trees cast shadows by starlight.
Nothing moves.
No flashlight,
everything we need to see
seen.
We stop, dog and me,
mesmerized
by Milky Way
brushed thin on arch of pale glitter
from horizon to horizon.
Even dog stares into illuminated stillness.
Seven sisters over Jupiter
tip Littler Dipper upside down
spilling light into our darkness.
Then we hear it,
cold calling us from four corners.
Half creaks
muted pops
from inside trees.
Frozen moisture trapped inside wood
pushes outward
stretching rigid life
demanding it change, expand.

"Ert" "Crk"
   "Trtk."
Dog's ears perk
   head tilts

13

first left then right
   then up then down.

Moments unroll
   sounds, dog, me,
      all one
with snow, stippled light,
piercing cold.

Stillness
the voice of winter's night
lingers.

Chickadee

A swollen chickadee clutching wire,
plump sphere of winter fat
inside a puffball of feathers,
she is a blowfish of the air.
Why does she not freeze in the envelope of wind
now icing taut window glass?

From late stick season
all the way through the annual ice age,
her song infiltrates my winter hermitage.
All other singers are gone.
Trees naked, earth hardened white,
fields perforated with brown straw –
my solitary winter cell
bereft of music if not for her.

Sure, crows scraw
and jays snat, pilfering
winter silence with urgent noise. Not music.
Chickadee stays, and sings.
Her song is faded now, summer bravado
awaiting release.
Still, when the sun is warm upon the snow
and sky a hopeful blue,
she sings.

In a world falling headlong down the chute
of economic quantifiers, imprisoned
within the narrows of merciless cost-benefit analysis,
thin quiet moments become rare –

an endangered species inside my heart.
The small unwitting warrior, that chickadee's song,
lifts me to a new, more primordial
definition of value.

Chromosome Reach

In low buttery light
a four day old sleeps
nestled on the soft pillow of my thorax.
His perfectly smooth head
radiates warmth.
Against intention, my fingers
nearly as long as his legs,
wander back again and again
to stroke that exquisite softness.
The knuckled front of my wrinkled maniples
scarcely brush the side of his head,
curling down
behind meticulously curved ears.

His face, oh –
artfully sculpted to be his and his alone.
Bulbous eyelids seamlessly rolling
into a tiny nose, skin
curling with soft lines
into lips, and that funny
heel-of-bread chin
with the weight of fleshy cheeks
puckering around it.
I want to close my eyes too
but they refuse to eclipse the little man
baking warm strength of life
into me.

Only days from sixty-five
with the years and miles aching
in my joints,
the limits of years
pressing upon my mind,
this sleeping infant heals me.
By osmosis, the stem cells
of new life seep through the moment
to renew my heart,
my brain, my bones.

Is it my chromosomes –
the genes of my father and mother
echoing, whispering through flesh
and running through my veins?
Or simply life itself, unrolled
and animated
with what we cannot name
or measure?

Rain

Rain.
The gwasher lands loudly on the kitchen roof yet sprinkles
so lightly as to animate single blades of grass.
Each drop a ratio
of weight to velocity.
Composed of individuals yet
spoken of as one, drops to rain
are as waves to ocean.

Desert-dwellers learn
to live without it, and with urgency
when it comes all at once, flooding
wadis and arroyos.
Where monsoon season reigns, rain
punishes and oppresses even as it rescues and saves.
Here among lakes and vineyards, neither
want nor waste scars the land
or life.

I Want to be Mary Oliver

I want to be Mary Oliver.

Oh to write poems on a stick
and have them tell stories
plain as my face in the pond,
see my spare words raise goose bumps
rendered as they are
in fortunate, quirky sequence.

When I write like her
mud will be an elixir and geese speak French,
a stone I find along the road
will tell me a nursery rhyme.

When Mary Oliver enters my soul –
an invisible current in the dark river of loss
a cattail will croon in a voice
we know all too well.
"Find your life," it will whisper,
and I will know for certain
a bear, a grasshopper,
the grasshopper in the palm of my hand I mean,
and a crow
all intend for me to lead a life
like the one I never had.

Stick Season

The city of trees surrounding my house
is a ghost town now, clawing naked
limbs, save the oak
whose amber leaves curl and shimmy, clenched
ferociously and shaking
against arctic blasts
thundering off the lake rattling the house.
Those crisp brown fists quiver
in the passing harpoons of air, yet even
the adolescent twigs springing from her core
hold steady, sturdy,
indifferent
to wind-chill, ice, or ricocheting squirrels.
Bushy evergreen escorts on three of her sides,
the oak stands sentry – pencil straight
with gnarled feet
buried under a lumpy carpet of snow.

It is not for me to know when
her leaves will drop, or why
pine needles hold bristle to brush, or if
anything dies
or lives.

Visiting After Winter

Behind the river birch at my window
April fisher-folk hook spawning silver perch
from dulled aluminum boats rigged with soft swivel chairs
and sonar contraptions flashing images of fish lurking below.

River birch peel, shed crisp flaps
of onionskin, revealing a raw
reddish complexion.
The birch bark waved at the house all winter
only to blow away in this mild spring air.

Meanwhile at the mouth of the river, winter beaver
decimated the grove of silver birch,
the thicket now a catastrophic mess of fallen
and wounded trees. Left
for humans to clean it up.

But here, from the warm side of the window,
in the worn leather chair I missed while escaping the snows,
it all melds – slender graceful river birch
with rotund and fallen silver birch
with hidden beaver
and the doddering boats
and fish.

Flesh Failures

This is a poem about skin drying,
flesh loosening – curdling
and hanging even.
Maybe too, about bone rubbing bone
the weight of them all
compressing down
tighter and smaller.

Six-feet-seven inches
at my zenith, then arches
I never knew were there, fell.
Those small bridges over air
unseen in our shoes,
who knew they added height?
One inch disappeared.
Eroding cartilage took away another.
Spine, knees, hips maybe,
each of them pop and scrape.
Down to six-foot-five.

My father was the tallest man I knew,
a mere six-three seemed giant to me then.
But he was lean where I am thick,
and shock-white Gary Cooper hair
on the place I shave beach grass to a sheen.
I could find him in any crowd –
comfort to a small boy.
Disconcerting it was then, to visit over the years
and find him smaller and smaller.
Not only did I outgrow him

he withered all the way down
to six feet.
Still, at ninety-three he was substantial
and strong, flailing
as a hematoma in his skull
pushed out reason, function
finally life.

We move on
diminishing day by day
as if nothing is happening.
Sweating on elliptical machines, grunting
with weights up and down up and down,
grimacing anxiously over carbs and sugar.
All a desperate grasp, clutching
a lifeline attached to the pier –
wave after wave relentlessly pulling,
tidal strength undiminished
ours becoming less and less capable
of holding on.

I lied.
This poem is not about skin.

HUMAN NATURE

Alone Again at the Wok 'N Roll

The dry voice of my dead father whispers into silence
"get your elbows off the table."

Sunday night, eight pm
sixty years old
flab weeping over a frayed brown belt
bellybutton kissing the edge of pale yellow Formica
freckled with the crust of earlier diners.
    Alone again at the Wok 'N Roll.

Regretting grizzly meat
glazed in sticky sauce, now sour on my tongue
a wad of silt in the urban river of my bowels.
I sit and stare at nothing
under flickering florescence casting
this earnest décor
in the yellow of dirty teeth.

I am waiting.
Nothing, no one
waits for me
anywhere.
A noodle
a cashew
a gnawing hope left on plastic plate –
someone, anyone
come.

No one does
and no one will
and here I am
alone again
at the Wok 'N Roll.

All that is left is a fortune cookie, small lifeless
prophet in a bag.
But it is a message in a bottle someone
somewhere, wrote to me.

Cellophane crackles
over currents of fusty air
as I unfold the ribbon of paper.
Mouth agape I read, "Pick new fortune cookie."

Depression

When the soul is weary
and toes curl on a heavy anchor
even going to the grocery is a final exam.
Once there, if you managed to go,
decisions about onions or grapes
butter or margarine
feel as harsh as Hobson's choice.

So many things belly the soul down
as if water in a balloon:
loneliness
grief
failure
remorse…each
a heaviness made of emptiness.

Before the balloon bursts
the mind droops to the floor
taking the body down with it.
Once there,
at the worst moment to decide,
it is get up and live
or give in and die.

Sunset Interrupted

An endless herd of waves pushes northward
as the hard breath of winter rattles glass,
still they cannot steal my gaze from the sun, atomic yellow
thinly veiled yet barely dulled
by a skim-coat of atmosphere. Too soon
it will ease down and hide away
behind a tungsten blue horizon.

The dog's dirty-blonde muzzle tipped
with a dark wet bulb, nuzzles
my hand — this writer's hand, writing.
"Play," she shouts, her long soft proboscis
wedged open with a slimy red toy.
"But the sun," I whine into her glassy almond browns,
"I need to capture it."

My words are meaningless jibber-jaw
in her perky ears. She nuzzles again, a wee bit
harder this time. "Come on, play!"

How often will I get to behold
a sunset like this? How many times
must I throw this stupid rubber ball?
Am I really talking to the dog?

Sunset and dog disappear.

Suddenly now, I am taken up in thoughts of you.
The skin of years wraps us

in a nearly single life, awkward
as we move against one another out of sync,
dancing to the same song we hear differently.
Still, I love you.

Two stones smoothed into one by the shoreline –
granular events grinding, rubbing,
tumbling us raw
then drying us out, salt stinging
then cleansing
only to reveal our brilliant colors and
soft earth tones too.

I do not always love you well,
just as my writing does not paint the breathless joy
of this sunset, nor my words grasped
by this silly dog. Still,
I love you, and love you still.

Moon

I
Today I am a quarter moon –
the universe having taken a bite out of me.
Do you ever feel like that?
Of course not, I am
alone.

II
A quarter moon is better
than no moon.

III
A quarter moon,
bright in the darkened sky
is still enough
to light the night
and lead me
home.

IV
Which god invented the quarter moon –
the chintzy, cheapskate one?

V
Quarter moon
half-moon

full moon –
it's not about me after all,
is it?

Conversion Therapy

To an extravert
the whole world is a mirror,
our own image in everyone we see.
Do they like my shirt?
Is my stomach sticking out?
Zipper up?
Do they like me?
It is exhausting.

I want to be an introvert
so I don't give a shit
what you think.
(And if I do,
you will never know).

Washington Street Cemetery

Little bone white tablets
lean backward, silent to the wind
unresponsive to creaking ancient trees,
flat-faced indifference to memory-driven squirrels
now clawing, manic for brunch held within crusty snow.

Some headstones look smooth,
alabaster polished by more than a century
of snow, rain, wind,
dogs
none an indignity to the dead.

The words etched into one are Latin,
a college professor, of Latin.
Was he insistent all generations going forward
know who and what he was, or
was it his children?

The smaller ones cry out
half eaten by earth heaving upward
or drowning in layers of humus.
They cover babies, the young
not deserving of a full-sized stone
in a world in which even the dead
are sorted by class.
Mr. So-and-So, "and his wife"
without a name,
get an erect obelisk

shadowing the lesser stones below - a gnomon
silently imposing sociological order
among the graves.

The dead do not care
about size or place or honor,
any more than a sycamore cares
about the height of a spruce
or the girth of an oak.
The cemetery whispers relentless
neurotic fixations
from those yet to die.

Or

It's the goddamn fork in the road –
the cleft between
left or
right, gain or
loss, yes or
no.

It is the moment you choose
to get pushed to the side, or
wander indifferently, or
shoot free-throws
to decide.

Your decision reaped
from missing information
is a crapshoot.
Vermin on the yellow line
bug juice on the windshield
collateral damage in body bags –
victims all
of fatal picks.

Dither as you will
sooner or
later
you walk forward or
backward, east or
west, up or
down.
The hammer of fate falls

immediately
when you decide –
the nauseating thud
you won't hear or
know
until least expected, or
desired most.

Behind Closed Eyes

When skin crawls
on the inside, and thoughts flit branch to branch
a winter brown goldfinch pecking for seed

when the longest
deepest, exquisitely practiced yoga breath
exhales an inert sigh

when it is five a.m.
with stained memories frozen
on the black box stage of an emptied cranium
it is time.
It is time to step into the deepest
darkest shadow,
and discover who or what
lives there.
"Hello, anybody home?"
You say it with innocence
in case they suspect something.
Enter, shake hands or paws
with what lives within.

If it is fierce and smelly, nod then get the hell out.
If it is seductive and smirks, be guarded.
If it is deadbeat and depressed, listen.

Behind closed eyes, in shadows
wakefulness never reaches,
skulk citizens with a vote.

Abbey of the Genesee

Monk's gait
scissors the distance between us, seizing
my stare, rapt in his rhythm
      step, swish, step, swish, step...

He's walking toward me, still a mile
down the road beyond the pond,
alfalfa and fairy-waves of heat between us.

He walks on the other side of the road, coming closer.
Velocity without lift, white robe rippling
edges of his brown scapula fluttering, a ghost of a breeze
I cannot feel –
      step, swish, step, swish, step...

Twenty-seven shades of green and counting
cross-legged atop my rock:
cattail
spruce
willow
grasses and grasses and grasses
cottonwood
jack pine
corn
milkweed
clover
broadleaf
ragweed
fern
bog stalks

that pungent sweet alfalfa —
Red-winged blackbird flitting in
and out
the window
of my vision.

Bullfrog plays banjo deep in his throat,
plucking philosophical questions, hidden
in unmown jungle of weeds collaring
the pond.

Monk now quarter mile away, diminished
grace in exchange for vigor.
Does he notice me,
perched on this sentinel stone?
Does he hear
the song of his own gait
   step, swish, step, swish, step?

Frog leaps from invisibility, apoplectic.
Redwing Blackbird hops straight up, a pogo stick leap
suspending her search for worms.
Some small javelin of sound spooked the close encounter
between their two species.

Now Mourning Dove moans to my left.
Monk approaches, gait still scissoring distance
still holding my eyes rapt in its rhythm.
He passes my rock
   step, swish, step, swish, step…

We do not speak.

Memories of Smell

I lost it.
Smell is gone but my nose
remains, even bigger now.
Watermelon seed nostrils
breathe every scent
over prickly nerve endings
that refuse their mission to dance.
They lie flat in the dark,
greased hair unable to sense.
What passes over them
is not felt, registers
no sensation –
no thing
nothing.

Sharp memories stab
the cortex from underneath
then bore a tunnel for the memory of smells
to rise up as if present-tense.
I remember Ngorongoro crater –
acrid earth, pungent hippopotami
soaking in their own shit,
baboon musk.
It all comes back apropos of nothing,
walking down a street in Buffalo, New York
in July – or the sweet scent
of fresh cut grass
on a winter morning
while starting the car.

But the scent of my baby's diaper I do not remember.
No drop of sweat
or adolescent stink
from any of my four children
do I remember.
The gods of smell left me at the altar
before my children were born.

Challenging Jesus

It just occurred to me,
that you and I, Jesus,
might have a different point of view.
Not that I would contradict you
publicly, or even presume
to be correct. Still,
I hold my ground, this
is what I think.

The first time I will
probably forgive someone's abuse,
lie, manipulation, treachery,
harm.
The second time, I probably won't.
The third time that dog is toast.

Just to grind it down
to a smooth, glassy lens,
I may do the forgiveness thing —
seventy times seventy even —
but not trust, not
an ounce.
Work with the scum, perhaps,
but not be vulnerable,
brook no opportunity to abuse me
again.

This is what I will do:
recognize what the bastard
or bitch is capable of,

watch them from a distance,
leave them to be the way they are,
and tell others
to be aware.

Forgiveness is not that hard, Jesus,
but reconciliation is a beast.
Harmless as a dove, wise
as a serpent – isn't that what you said?
Well, rattlesnakes
are toxic, and
no matter what you say, I don't
play with them.

Existential Truth

Blue streaked tongues of yellow flame
fed by invisible gas
infiltrates real-looking wood
made of non-consumable synthetic something.
The proximity of fire
fills my head more than warms
my body.

A blond Labrador
mixed with Golden Retriever,
a faux breed of canine yet real and shedding
presence, sleeps curled
in front of the real but fake fire.

This world
is difficult to discern.

The brilliant morning sun
reaches through dirty glass, warming
my face from billions of miles away.
The fire, two feet to my left, is a distant
breath of warmth to my barren ankles.
Reality television
emanates from the White House
as real bodies die
around the actual world
for fake causes

at the command
of an unreal president
lambasting fake news.

It is a real fire
fueled by genuine gas
whooshing through a manufactured straw of steel,
sucking across hundreds of miles
only to lick these imitation logs
producing real warmth
that does not truly heat much of anything.
Meanwhile,
existential truth, real
meaning – if ever there was such a thing –
seems hard to find.

I studied truth
many years ago, and found it
among the gathered leaves of books. It escaped,
and remains elusive
on this side of the veil
where I live with real imitations
and authentic trickery
and manufactured reality.

Cup O' Joe at the End of the World

Inside this ashen shroud
empty of birds,
barren of trees
the clock ticks
then tocks
toward apocalypse.
The edges of time are burnt crust,
the once endless promenade of seconds
diminished to a residue of granules slipping
between pinched curves
of this now unholy hourglass.

My craving, the gnawing rat in my stomach,
is only for one cup of coffee.

Waiting at the end of the world,
with so much to lust for
or savor in the dawning darkness,
I crave only a hot mug to wrap my fingers around
full to the brim, wisps of steam
dancing on black glass.

Simplicity.

Perhaps if we had stuck to simple things
then teetering here at the brink,
waiting for nothingness
to pour into emptiness
when the lights go out, our demise

would not be so certain. Had we been content
with the goodness of a hot cup of coffee,
this would not be the period at the end of the

THE SACRED

Cairn
/kern/

I smile at the small pile of stones,
horn-shaped tower of homely flat rounded rocks
stacked leaning,
straight or curling.
Variegated not bright, from sandy
to dark gray to black
streaked with white
and sparkle-infused garnet.
Ungainly yet friendly,
no comeliness
unless you were anxious
and in search of one.

Awkward silent fairies
is how I think of them –
stone whispers of kindness
left to echo in the ear of anyone
who comes along.
Cairn offer assurance
about the path you are on – your trace
still aligned.
They smile and say, "cross here in safety"
when water parts the land.
Eloquent even on barren rock
or dessert sand
empty of anything else to speak,
or poking through the hushed silence of snow.

Connotation or denotation
they point the way,
and who doesn't need that
from time to time?

September Butterfly

Is there anything so lonely as a September
butterfly or bee, wafting
up and
down, in
and around
dead clover, dried grass?

Here now, from my wooden bench, I see
buttery yellow wings catch light
and blend sweetly
with the tittering yellow leaves of poplars, the breeze
breathing heavy through the trees, a sashay
of colors reaching for crescendo
before death.

Then, as if
shot like a canon, I see
the blue orb of Earth all alone
in deep space, wobbling
slightly off her orbit, the way an autumn butterfly
lilts and quavers, up and down
over brown grass.

My Father Died Last Night

My father died last night.
His body long as a casket
gaunt as a heron
gnarly as roots
soon buried beneath the shade of a pin oak tree.

My father died last night.
I held his hand and watched his neck
a tiny bluish tick under paper thin skin
suddenly melt to stillness.

Ninety-two years he was a river of blood.
His Indiana father coursing through time
to my New York children
as surely as the Wabash is a varicose vein
meandering from Ohio to Illinois.

My father died last night.
Tomorrow the earth swallows him,
smothered by the same dry, thirsty grass
covering his mother and father and wife, and secretly,
the ashes of his old dog.

My father died last night.
At home in his bed by the window,
his long carpentering fingers lacing mine
still larger in death
than my own fingers warmed by life.

Flux

PHYSICS – the rate of flow of a fluid, radiant energy, or
particles across a given area.

Look the universe in the eyes.
Your lover stares back.
Gaze. Penetrate
those black pools – veils
over alien probes.

Flat-footed on the crest of your life
survey the blue green distant hills, which is
the iris of your lover's eye.
See the wild animal
looking back,
coming for you.

Even a tree, stare at it.
Any tree, leprous sycamore
or hunchback birch.
The look I mean
begins in your stomach
among writhing bacteria
but lower, tunneling up
from tubes of pitch darkness
where life festers.
Open it. Twist
open the valve
feel energy squeeze up the tube

into your eyes.
Now it flows out
fusing you with the tree.

We are not condemned
to a three-by-six cell of flesh.
Solipsism be damned.
Nihilism is dead.
Open from the inside out,
release that thin current
arcing now
with some other stream of life.

Physiology of Truth

Blossoms sprout in pain.
Suckling on rival truths
will simmer the blood, roil
the heart, and grow
life.

Binary truth pinches an artery
parching its Siamese twin, cursing both
with failure to thrive.
Lulled into complacency, singular truths
starve us to death.

But cradling two opposing truths
within the same buttercup,
each bare face flowering above tender shoots,
wicks nectar up stamens of loss, weeping
both pain and light.

Faith
no less than love
no less than hope
no less than all things that matter
writhe.

This is the beginning of
wisdom.

Listening to Dark Angels

Dark angels –
eels in dank corners
on thrones of wrong
haunting wakefulness, hibernating the in-between.
I unlock the door.

I am listening.

We might have been best of friends
on another day, different night
if not for scuffling
over the same body –
fighting for the driver's seat.

I am listening.

Brighter angels let me down
preening in the spotlight
ogling in the mirror.
I listened to them.
They still have an ear
but now I will listen to you.

I am listening.

This inscape of ours shifted
land-shear and rockslides
collapsed boundaries
converged continents.
We can't keep marking

the same corners as our own.
I am letting you out.

If you start swinging your weight
pushing the weak
tricking the stupid
baiting the earnest
I'll slam you down
then put you back
faster than a snake bite.

I am listening,
for now.

The Moment of Recovery

She saw me from her distance
across days and highways,
weeks and airmiles.
All the while she cataloged explanations
that did not fit
excuses too small to cover
times I said I would call
but didn't.

She named it with a question
only I could answer.
Her voice was grainy with distance
through the landline
hammered with a tone of knowing –
grave unspoken understanding.

Looking back from across
the wide ocean of sobriety
years and a lifetime later –
even a different life –
I wonder if she knows
it was her voice
and her words
at that moment
that drew the key
into a rusty lock
opening my liquid cell.

I might have told her once
when she called out of the blue

years later and well into my marriage
when I was afraid to talk.
But I don't remember.
If not, "thank you."

This is what we are.
Pointillist paintings, thousands of flecks,
colors brilliant and pale, stabbed
by hands not our own
on a canvass
not of our own making.

Passion

A random curl of air
wafts above dusty gray ashes.
One red eye opens beneath the glaze of ash,
then another
then another.

Ex nihilo, a yellow bud of flame
licks the air
held from flight by a pinch of blue.
In a blink, a hundred
red eyes open
eating away ashen silt
becoming lava stones engulfed by fire.

This is the beginning of passion.

Cinders of anger glowing hot
with reddened coals of compassion,
sweating among embers of indignation
dripping with molten tongues of yearning, all restless
beneath a glaze of ordinary moments.
Flammable
explosive
ready to ignite
all of it fed by one small breath.

War, heroism
brutality
insurgency, love

sexual ecstasies
and exquisite kindnesses,
all incarnations
of the same
human flame.

Memory

Wandering around on the inside
we are the only ones gawking into wakefulness
at low-hanging stars
sparkling amidst the internal darkness.

Inside, within this strange universe
everyone looks just as they did, and me too.
Old girlfriends visit along with
drunken whirlies in the night
missed opportunities
tearful fits of laughter
trophies earned or captured
deep, wet kisses
scalpeled words, shame-filled deeds
the night your ship came in
the hour death ushered away your mother
ten thousand Bic lighters flickering teardrops in a stadium
a shiny black bicycle under the tree
that day your own dark shadow hit bottom...
All there, distant stars
twinkling from sapphire darkness
a heaven so easy to look at, impossible to pluck,
never again to visit.

"What is this poem about,"
my twelve-year old daughter asks. "Wait a few years,"
I say, "you'll know."

Run-on Sentences Above a Fragile Ocean

(Cape Breton meditation)

When even an ocean seems fragile
when, standing above thunderous waves spewing
rubble from roar, broken stones
and empty shells mere pennies at your feet,
and still you can imagine how it becomes a dead sea
when, in your mind's eye, looking
upon steel blue behemothian depths, and still
you can imagine a barren womb, hollow of life
when, standing otherwise at peace with the salty breeze
glazing your cheeks, the Spielberg in your brain
removes those angry waves, and in a flash imagines
the landscape a redox of craters lined with dust,
there is a sudden clarity that the coming devastation
is a bitterness rendered by unsustainable pleasures, the swill
of whoring consumers and sultans.
Then, when you can imagine waste on that scale,
the balloon of modernity is punctured by the sharp pin
of a small human brain, its vast
science unsheathed and shriveled
then, when you can imagine beyond the power of Salvation
to the inevitable death of the ocean
then, when you are on your own, free-falling
between the plank and a grave, in limbo
between post-modern and pre-wisdom
when you know, when it is cut like an x
into your heart of hearts, that Earth is terminal

when you sit above a rocky tree line, beholding
the vista of a millennial forest with its shocking green,
a comforter blanketing Mesozoic mountains
as so much moss on a river rock, and you know
all those lives you see and even the ones below the catchment
            of your vision
are cellmates on Death Row

when, as if from a god's-eye view, you see
a tear running down the face of the moon, and Earth's blue-
white swirl of atmosphere dissolving like tired suds in a sink,
the third planet from the sun, caked
before your eyes with crimson dust

when, even further down the cylinder of death,
you see the once bucolic Earth explode, break apart
land in pieces, on other planets or
melted by stars, and slurped into a black hole

then, then the covers of religion are pulled off
in the cold night of the soul. Then, shivering
alone on your bed, naked
you will decide there and then, whether
to pull covers over your head or take a slow deep breath
and release other options into your imagination

knowing that from now on, either way,
sleep will be fitful.

When, on a shirtless day, carefree
beneath celestial warmth pouring down
upon every pimple and pore of your smiling skin,
you know without thought

the sun that returned Icarus to Earth,
the same sun that burned crow
and made him black forever,
will itself be a cinder smoldering in space

when you can squint and see
the sun's photosynthetic kiss on every blade of grass,
and every sugary red-stemmed maple leaf
and you know all days are numbered

when you know the vast expanse of interstellar space
offers no eternity, that Adam ate
from the Tree of Knowledge of Good and Evil
instead of harvesting the Tree of Life,
and you can see the sun for what it is –
a non-renewable resource
soon to sputter and cough and burn out
with a bad smell

that is when
you will have been left alone
to play blind-man's bluff in the hallway of eternity.

That is when you know, even if you were to remove
the blindfold, there will still be nothing to see.

That is when, and only when,
you will have arrived
at the beginning of thought.
In the dark of eternity,
at the bottom of the well,
there is nothing, or only, trust in God.

Mother Teresa's God

A response to the revelation that Mother Teresa reached out in vain for forty years to be touched again by a God she encountered only once in personal revelation, and even then, only to send her into the streets of Kolkata.

I know you
who left that old woman out to dry
fried soul bacon crisp
from inside out

I know you
who left us stranded here
cynicism replacing grief
gangrenous in the Hundred Acre Wood

I know you
who shimmers on glassy water
never held never touched never heard
never known

I know you
who gags mystics with intimate fingers
swilling blood and tears
they starve swallowing

I know you
who snarls orders backstage
Oz-words on stone and papyrus
cocktails of bile and milk

I know you
who jilted the wrinkled nun and others –
lunatic in crown of thorns
Baptist preacher shot in head

I know you
keep your distance
I will not be known
by you

I know you.

The Unseen Visible
Seen by the Invisible Unseen

You see me.

Seeds of scions sprout
between your toes, matriarchs
and patriarchs: Abrahams, Isaacs, and Jacobs –
the mitochondrial Eve
        but still you see me.

Me, a mite, mere fleck of stardust
invisible, infinitesimal
soft matter
grain of sand
smidgeon
dab
crumb
alloyed speck of mush –
        you see me.

Me, nearly nothing.
You, utterly everything.
        You see me,
hear my whine
know my voice

faint heartbeat buried in my ribs
whispers to you, and you hear it
among waves lapping the sands
of the Cosmos.

Dream

Halfway in
          and halfway out
squeezed in the middle
by a dream-catcher.

Lowered here by sleep
into this floppy dimension
where chairs are wobbly and misshapen,
people wear wrong faces, all of it
oddly pleasurable in the way of a sneeze.
Here in this twixt-and-between –
walls not always hardened
skies not always up
Earth not always down –
          I wander.

Once, stuck like this,
I heard the voice of God
tell me, "Go."
          I went.

Now I hear nothing
in this warp
where time and sleep and
          wakefulness meet.

Spiritual not Religious

Sultry blond sits near my feet
a coy ninety-degree angle looking back
over her shoulder, big brown eyes
daring me not to touch – begging me to draw near.

My dog – I call her mine but of course, she is not –
was diagnosed as spiritual-not-religious in a recent survey.
She may be neither. Mindfulness is not a choice for her.
She charges eagerly into each moment embracing every angst,
          rabbit, squirrel,
and existential meaninglessness
with exactly the same hundred percent of corpuscles
blasting blood through her entire body.
Can such mindlessness be mindful?
Can a brain immune to monkey-mind
held delightfully between perked ears,
be anywhere other than in the moment?

Meanwhile, can I be spiritual while committing an act
        of religion?
What would it be if I was mindful, inhaling through my nose
and exhaling through my mouth
with perfect diaphragmatic stillness,
seamlessly woven into the present moment while sitting on
        a wooden pew?
Would it be spiritual if curls of frankincense-infused smoke
shrouded distant men in pointy hats festooned in brightly
        colored robes
embroidered like my aunt Elma's couch?

Surrounded by the unnatural noise of air
pushed through trays of metal pipes and blasted out again,
am I spiritual or religious?
Is it one or the other, or is it
simply like my dog who only knows to wag her tail in any
        moment?

My Dog and God

My dog and God, are difficult
to understand.

So often dog stares, a forlorn
tilt of the head, eyes hopeful.
Yet she must know by now –
so much inaction from me – she will get nothing.
I look down and wonder what she wants.
Hearing no words, and seeing
no further gestures, I go on
emptying the dishwasher
or writing this poem.

God wants something too,
but hearing silence and not seeing
so much as a cute dog face from God,
I go on brushing out the toilet
and grocery shopping.

Look, if you guys
want something,
say so.

The Lord is my GPS

If I put my hoodie on backwards now
what will I do when I'm eighty-five?
My father, who fell to his death at 93,
couldn't hear a lick. Do I get to hear
my great grandchild cry?
My mother, who gradually suffocated
when fifty years of nicotine juice
penetrated the bulkhead to her lungs,
feared aloneness at the end. Will I be riddled with anxiety
when death, smirking victor it is, takes my hand?

The Lord is my shepherd
who tells me nothing, expects
me to follow blindly, shares
little by way of the future.
Would I prefer that God be my GPS
and break it all down for me?
Every twist and turn of the road
spelled out in language I could read,
a voice with an accent I could choose?
No.

Declan's Birth

Where do tears come from?
I do not mean lacrimal glands —
don't be so literal.
I mean joy.
I mean awe.
Wordless stuttering
over sweet goodness beyond taste
touch, knowledge.

As a man, and I speak
for all of them,
childbirth is at a distance.
Even when we are right there
in the room, Doula or no,
blood on the floor
scent of soil from mulched innards
urine and sweat,
it is an out of body experience.
Not our body, always
hers.

Still, we were there
in the beginning, like a god
igniting life in the dark.
But the earth formed in her womb —
cells dividing in warm shallow water.
Bedrock and tree limbs growing out of sight
inside her.
We mattered at first
but not again until

the glistening waterbaby
in a sheath of muddy excretions
breathes air.

Only a grandfather now
hundreds of miles away
and thirty years from that day
my daughter squirmed from the tunnel.
This photograph of his minutes-old face
is a meaningless digital reproduction on a phone
no more tactile than glass.
Still, tears.

A hand throttles my throat
I choke and stutter.
Warm beads of water sting —
eyes blinking
tears rolling.
Something,
that thing I cannot name,
collapses the miles
the years
the gendered distance
into inches.

CAIRN

Essays Marking the Trace

A Note to the Reader

It will not take much imagination to pull a thread or two connecting these essays with one or more the previous poems. Some of the essays were intentional experiments aimed at looking differently at the same subject from another written form. Others were simply accidental and more likely indicate my rapt fascination with the subject matter.

Many years ago, I wrote a weekly column for a church publication with a required limit of five hundred words. For the past three years, I have had the pleasure of writing a weekly newspaper column with the same limit. In between, I taught a college course in religion for five years in which any writing assignment was limited to five hundred words on the theory that in the student's future, few employers would ever want them to write more – and probably much less.

My longest poem is six hundred words, but most of them hover around one-hundred and fifty. Poems feel tight and spare in comparison to writing sermons that run from sixteen hundred to twenty-five hundred words, which nudges the essay into the cozy middle. When I want to challenge myself, I transform a Sunday sermon into a thoroughly secular version at five-hundred words for the newspaper.

I hope reading poems and essays on the same or similar subjects, offers the reader a unique and interesting experience that also serves as an invitation to visit their own experiences from a variety of perspectives. It turns out that how many words we use to describe and share a moment, may actually shape how we behold it.

May these essays be cairn along your trace. May they encourage you forward.

"Getting Intimate with a Tree"
Northeast Kingdom, Vermont

Deserts are magnificent and spectacular – a landscape once seen
that will hollow you out and crawl inside to take up residence.
The same with rocky shorelines or undulating beaches along
sun-soaked coasts. It is easy to grasp why certain topography
and flora evoke a sense of home for people – I feel that way
about the flat expanse of freshly ploughed fields in the
Heartland when the fragrance of moist rich soil permeates the
air.

But I need trees.

I need lots of trees, particularly the chaotic diversity of a
deciduous forest. Four distinct and rigorous seasons flavor a
forest of maple, oak, birch, pine, and fir carpeted underneath
by a luscious riot of ferns and wildflowers melting year to year
into a spectacularly fertile soil.

Trees are gods.

No, I'm not a Druid nor crazy. But truly, have you ever stared
at a tree long enough to see its soul? Have you ever put your
face inches from a tree as if it were your lover's face and felt the
energy between you? No? Well, go try it.

In my yard, just beyond the window where I often write, stands
an oak flanked by three spruces. Not far away three river birch
spread their beauty; more reddish than their cousin the silver
birch, and they shed year round with strips of paper bark

jittering in the wind. The oak hangs onto her leaves all winter, curled fists of brittle brown parchment quavering yet holding tight through the fiercest winter gales that rush down the mountain and across the lake doing their best to scatter them.

Each of these trees, like any tree, has a unique personality accessible for getting to know. That is the key of course, getting to know a tree well enough to discern its character. As with any intimacy, knowledge comes from experience – touch, smell, sound, sight, and even taste if you dare. And time. Time is the yeast of relationship with a tree.

Living together through seasons and knowing how each one makes it through winter, drinks up spring, thrives in summer, and prepares through autumn is the knowledge that grants the kind of relationship I am intimating here. Because trees move so slowly, breathe so silently, and change so subtly most of the time, it is not like learning to know a dog or a human. It requires much more curiosity on our part, much more active solicitation and rigorous perceiving.

I am particularly close to the oak, a kind of rugged friend through thick and thin. The river birch are women at the bar I flirt with. There is a willow at the edge of our property I whisper to as I ride nearby on my John Deere. At the corner of our house is a dwarf ornamental who is crabby in an endearing way.

I could go on but you likely think I am nuts as it is. All I can say, when we take the time to know a tree, to learn its character and discern its spirit, something good will happen.

"Rime Ice Around the Heart"
Northeast Kingdom, Vermont

When fog freezes over, not Hell, tiny droplets of water form a layer of white ice over whatever it touches. It is called *hard* rime ice. *Soft* rime ice is the same thing, except it is frozen by wind on the windward side of an object. Even though we are 98.6 degrees inside our bodies, our emotions can become frozen and covered in rime.

Almost any emotion, if we neglect it, can form a layer of numbing agent that will then seize up our complex network of emotions. Once formed, it becomes a hard or soft layer of distance. Some emotions don't even require neglect.

Grief does it naturally; just seeps in and coats everything inside and numbs us. It is good at first, when we are in pain from sudden loss. But if we allow grief to solidify it mucks things up. Normally grief melts in place naturally over the course of events, months and even years. Eventually, when grief has gone well, it is reduced to icy spots we slip on now and again – welling up with tears without the least warning and seemingly unconnected to anything in particular. But with neglect grief can harden and leave a deep freeze around the heart.

Anger, of course, is famous for such hardening of emotional arteries.

Anger hardens into an aggressive resentment or an inwardly pointed depression. Either way, one day we may suddenly recognize just how numb we have become, walled in by a frosty anger about something that has long since passed. It fills us with trepidation because the only way to go from oxygen-starved – inside where we live – to the vibrant world on the outside, is through it. Through the rime.

The only way out is through.

We have to go through all those feelings we neglected in the first place when we were avoiding the hurt. We never reach a point at which we want to hurt or grieve. Yet the only way out is through. When our emotional arteries are covered with a hard or even soft rime of anger, hate, resentment, grief, regret, shame, fear (you name it), the only way out is through.

If we reach for a substance to take the edge off, unbeknownst to us at the time, it actually makes things worse. The little buzz induced to soften what we have to go through actually hardens it. Worse, if we keep using something to soften the pain it actually takes us further and further away from the source. There is no bullet to bite, no analgesic or palliative to put us to sleep during surgery, only the caked-on film of previously avoided yuck we have to go back through in order to find our way out.

With all the sleep aids, anti-depressants, diet pills, legalized numbing agents, and illegal hollowing substances hawked and available, we simply will not be able to go through the pain we need to travel in order to recover a human society with a foreseeable future. We have already become hazardously numbed by those who pitch pharmaceutical relief and a cultural that generally encourages mental slumber, how much worse will it get as we create and market ever more powerful and distorting pills and "medications."

I sound like some kind of prudish crank tilting at windmills. No one in their right mind goes cold turkey against what hurts when they don't have to. Still that is what I am proposing. Face what hurts inside, feel it all the way through to the other side. It is not only our personal wellness at stake; our capacity to build and nurture a livable future depends upon it.

"Never Enough"
Quebec City, Quebec

A soul-singeing rant begins as a yelp or whine when something good just can't last but we want it to anyway.

In the bitter cold and spectacular beauty of Quebec City I bought a silly hat. It is a WWII bomber style hat with flaps lined with fake fur and a dome of fake leather. But it is oh-so warm. I got tired of my bald head and big ears being cold. Then, even though March had already arrived, I bought knee-high Mucks. It began as envy toward my brother's boots but was driven by exasperation with cold, wet feet as I walked the dog through drifts of snow each day. Finally, at the end of my second Vermont winter, my armor was complete.

Even so, under the star-strewn cupola above and with the deep silence of snow surrounding, I can only last so long in the sub-zero air. Ice forms on my eyelashes and the night air penetrates the slim gap between the bottom of my long coat and top of my tall boots. In spite of the cold I want to stay longer, savoring awe beneath a spiraling Milky Way speckled across the dark night.

Even the dog sits at attention, ears perked, patient but alert. We are silhouettes on the road where nothing is moving and any sound is muffled by a deep rounded carpet of white. Something or someone we cannot see is up there looking down and wonders about these two creatures and our nightly routine in the cold.

Honestly, this view of the universe is most intensely brilliant and clear on the coldest nights of winter when the digital signal on my phone screams minus five, ten, or even twenty. The summer view is great and more relaxing as we lounge on patio recliners and stare into the cosmos, but in winter the Big Dipper pours its spectacular mysteries on the end of my driveway. On the most frigid nights something about the bitter air is a sign that the thin vaporous veil between the rest of the solar system and us has become thinner.

But it is not enough.

Our few minutes alone with the miraculous cosmos spread out above us is not enough. The number of clear night skies without clouds or without the brilliant moon placing a pall of light between stars and us, is simply not enough. The summer evenings when stargazing and stupor feel limitless is not enough. It is just never enough.

Such is the human lament. Orgasm is too short, good wine runs out, the flavorful juiciness of steak disappears with the last bite, summer comes to an end, and the glassy goo-filled gaze between lovers evaporates into an ordinary moment much too soon. Never enough.

I know, I know. If it were any other way it would be disaster. Still, the taste or sensation or pleasure or view or music or aroma is never quite enough. Just a little more, *please.*

"Unpacking Wounds"
Newport, Vermont

"The wound is the place where light enters you."

Those are the words a friend texted me out of the blue. The words are Rumi's (and a hundred other Wise Ones speaking in scores of languages across thousands of miles and years).

"Sure do wish that light would make those wounds feel better," I smirked; though smirking is difficult to communicate in a text.

"It does," came an emphatic answer to my complaint.

"I guess I need to open them a little wider then," I added glumly as I looked out upon a gray day that began with a dusting of snow almost two weeks after the spring equinox.

Sometimes I get plain old weary — a weariness of soul.

Weariness is a universal human inevitability under certain conditions, but it is anguish only people of privilege can give into and survive. Imagine the exhaustion of those living in a war zone, in a civil war for example? Giving into exhaustion in such random and brutal circumstances almost guarantees death. Or imagine living in Tornado Alley with ominous dark clouds on the horizon? Being too weary to deal with it could be a permanent exit strategy.

Yet the news pecks away at us, drilling cavity after cavity and filling them with images and chatter of human maleficence, negligence, and just plain evil intent. It isn't the news media's fault that we do all this horrible stuff to each other and the environment, but the sources of information are so pervasive and its reporting is left running on an endless loop. Ignorance is far less wearisome.

But as I said, only those living in privilege could even think about giving into weariness if we wish to continue to live and hold out hope of thriving someday. Listening to NPR my weariness is poked by a story about the astounding endurance of an especially petite bird. The Blackpoll Warbler is a half-ounce of feathers airborne for three days above an ocean hungry for its failure. She pecks a loved-one goodbye in Nova Scotia or Cape Cod not to perch again until Venezuela; muscles and flesh no heavier than two twenty-five cent pieces and still she lands with a song in her throat.

The news is not good today, any more than it was yesterday. Today my wounds feel less like an opening for light and more like a repository for heaviness. But hearing about the Blackpoll Warbler opens the window so I can breathe a little better.

Just knowing of her miraculous migration buoys me.

So now I suspect there is an antidote to the crush of horrid news. It is to go looking for the rest of the stories, the ones that allow us to inhale wonder and exhale awe. It doesn't take away the suffering we know is there, or even our sense of impotence about our own part in it. But awareness of the amazing and miraculous offers a counter-balance, an infusion of remedy to the weariness brought by the other.

And now as I think about it, the reason my wounds haven't been letting in much light lately is because I cover them up. Snow or not, spring is here and time to pull the blinds and open the windows. I intend to land with a song in my throat, too.

"Loud Angels"
Geneva, New York

It is early morning dark.

A star or two smiles through the light pollution of white street lamps, the domed blaze of home security floods, and even the lunar sliver of light curled further above. Dog and I crunch brown, red, and yellow leaves, some the size of a catcher's mitt, in the historic cemetery where no one has been buried for a hundred years. Old, pale gravestones the color of the moon, are tongues rising up from the lumpy ground that wag left and right, forward and backward, and talk in whispers.

Even this early there is enough noise to wake the dead.

A garbage truck grinds its gears from one to three, a school bus lets loose the yellow blimp's distinctive flatulence, the car with the bad muffler that heads to work the same time each day, and that dog with an emphysema bark that yaps at us from the other side of the street. But we disappear into the cemetery and pull an invisible curtain of quiet behind us.

I wish people could visit one another's thoughts. Just fly in for a small look then zoom out again. If only we could do it, leave no footprint or debris behind, but peek in on a few special people to determine whether or not we are crazy. I don't know about you, but sometimes I feel the need for verification.

It is the angels that raise this question.

It is those angels of my better nature as much, if not more, than the darker ones that concern me. They whisper loudly in the echo chamber and lithely dance the tango on the tiniest of nerves. Most of the time I do not know which to believe, or even if any of them are trustworthy. I know for a fact that memories have been switched before, changed to conceal the guilty and sometimes to indict the innocent. They also lay blame-traps for other people to step in and hold elections about things for which they don't even have a vote. That rowdy crowd of voices would just as soon be in charge instead of me, and doggone if I do not always know which of us is in charge.

But the cemetery is quiet. Only the ghosts of other people, and long-ago ones at that.

Dog wants to get off leash and run crazy eights or chase the posse of bold squirrels that sashay around the cemetery making noise in the leaves, knowing she could never catch them. Her unadulterated joy of smelling everything sweet or nasty, and sheer delight in whatever moment she is in, causes me to suspect there are no angels lurking in her mind. Just whatever is there within the reach of her senses, and that appears to be enough for happiness. Oh, to be a dog some days, with a nose that works and soft, floppy ears that hear everything, and yet instinctively know what to pay attention to and what to ignore.

"Listening to Time"

Finger Lakes, New York

Feel it.

It is a rending of pressurized elements, the slight movement in tightly packed earth. There is a loosening amid bits of gravel, decaying pieces of wood, moisture that thawed and froze again all winter. It is difficult to know if the rending is a tearing apart, as when a newborn coerces and compels its mother's body to open for release. It could be more lithe, a supple green shoot making its way like water or tai chi, by way of least resistance.

Hear it.

It is tempting to kneel down, brush away brown leaves ugly upon the lumpy black topsoil of the garden, and hold an ear to the ground. The sounds are imaginable — a liquid squelching, suctioned kind of slithering through the deep space beneath our vision. What will be brilliant blossoms, sturdy vegetables, ordinary ground cover, and a chaos of greens, is now agitating upward toward the sun.

Fathom it.

A mere seven degrees on a Sunday morning, snow still insisting upon its place among us, and likely many more cold days and nights coming our way. Icy winds, sleet, slush, soggy damp cold all taunting us from their niche in the weeks ahead. Even so, it's coming.

Remember it.

Time-lapse photography captures a raw white bulb or little green shoot below the surface of the earth, looking like a salamander slithering, wiggling upward this way and that, a current of life insisting upon fresh air and sun. We have seen what it looks like by the magic of a digital camera, but we are left to trust what we cannot witness ourselves: spring is coming.

It is an equinoctial double-exposure, when two seasons overlap and we feel them both at one and the same time. The waves of spring begin lapping their way onto our shore, even as the waves of winter still pound the surf just before returning to the ocean of time.

Mostly we do not hear the ethereal echoes of eternity while living between seasons, not as we would while standing on a beach. Our deafness is because changing barometric pressures, wildly fluctuating temperatures, and shifting elements in the atmosphere jerk us around. But for those who take the time to feel it, hear it, and even imagine it, the dance of winter and spring offers a pleasurable window onto the elegance of time.

One indicator of a healthy mind, and one element of a spiritual practice, is the willingness and ability to listen to time. It can be done listening to ancient trees talk, reading the braille of igneous rock, meditating upon the flow of elderly rivers, and standing with feet collapsing in the sand as waves wash over them. The seasons speak to us also, if we listen. If we slow ourselves down and listen to the changes inching around us, we may hear the elegant wisdom of the seasons as it whispers through our days.

"The End"
Geneva, New York

If you read this column even occasionally, then you know my affinity for beholding trees, birds, water, the seasons, and discovering in the minutiae of relationships between them, some unexpected shimmering insight. We so often hold ourselves outside of nature, as if we are something distinct from the rest of creation, and so miss seeing ourselves in the glory and chaos all around. There is of course, a dark and stormy seam to seeing through that lens as well.

Once upon a time, I visited the end. I was on the edge, hunkered down in a primitive cabin on the rim of a cliff on Cape Breton Island, Nova Scotia. No running water or electricity, and literally, at the end of the last gravel road on the far edge of its northern most reaches.

For twenty-four hours or more, the sky above the ocean opened fire with lightning bolts, scattershot streaks and flashes stabbing the waves and the land. The wind shook the cabin and rain raked the house in sheets. When finally, there was a moment of calm on the battlefield, we wandered out to peer over the ledge.

Standing on the lip of the cliff gaping at the sea raging below, the waves against the rocks were so white it looked like milk. The ocean seemed even more immense than usual, angry and shouting its discontent with noises I had never heard before. To be sure, I had never witnessed the ocean from a wild place like that, nor seen it so wild with so little between me and it.

The sheer power of the ocean overwhelmed my rational mind and tingled every one of my senses. Then it happened.

In a flash, I saw the surface of Mars – instead of raging waves I saw dry, red dust frozen in airless space. I saw the end of life as we know it, there at the moment of the ocean's unassailable vitality. It was clear to me that one day, hopefully long beyond any of our lifetimes, the Earth would no longer be the blue-green beauty we know today. Just as clearly, I could see the culprit was our lust, our deadly consumeristic appetite that usurps all things to its own desire.

There would be no reprieve, no pardon from an Almighty God who insists on a happy ending. In my Jeremiah-like vision, the end was both judgment and logical conclusion.

As is being more widely reported now, Shell, Exxon, and the American Petroleum Institute had hard science in the 1960's for the catastrophic effects of continued and increased use of fossil fuels on climate and Earth's ecosystems. They knew it, hid it, and then funded the denial campaign and Tea Party candidates who championed denial, when the data began to surface.

Who are these people, these monsters behind the curtain of corporate America? What adjectives could possibly describe their jowly guard dogs populating the kennels of power in Washington, D.C.?

Well, just as we are able to garner insights about ourselves growing amid the other gems of nature, we can also see ourselves reflected among the death-eaters of American

business and politics. Truly, we have met the enemy and they
are us.

"When we stop is where we stop"
Finger Lakes, New York

Perhaps you have noticed that all around us our familiar institutions seem to be cracking and crumbling, or at best stumbling forward.

Educational institutions, for example, designed in the 19th century are straining to hold together – not unlike our hundred-year-old bridges bending beneath the weight of more traffic than ever imagined. Our two-hundred-year-old financial system is spawning things it can't control - the speed of wealth and capital transfer, and absence of national borders, seems to make some of its central elements irrelevant.

So many of our institutions and grand philosophies come to us from the 19th and early 20th centuries, but we are light years away from that pre-WWII world. They now represent the big ideas and eloquent rhetoric of a world dead and gone. Think of the intellectual, psychological, and imaginative distance between the world before Hiroshima and Auschwitz, and the world after them.

I am not talking about the physical world so much as the human perspective – the mind's eye.

Take just a moment to consider the difference between the political culture before the assassinations of JFK, MLK, Bobby, and Malcolm, and then the post-Nixon environment. Likewise, there is an un-crossable distance between perspectives on the human condition that existed prior to the Moonwalk and the one conceived under more current images of the polar ice shelf melting.

Even more profoundly, conjure up this difference in worldviews created by this contrast of experiences. In your left ear you are waiting several minutes for an operator to connect you with another party, and in your right hand, with your thumb, you post a tweet two thousand people on six continents will read within seconds.

My friends, those different worlds are as connected as a spinal fracture exposing a thin strand of nerve. The distance is so great it has utterly changed the human mind and what the brain sees and imagines. But there is a tectonic rupture we haven't truly recognized yet.

In this moment in the history of humankind, we have at least three centuries of human mindset double and triple exposed one on top of the other. At one and the same time, looking around the world and even in our own country, we have people living under the assumptions of the 19th century, with others living within the worldview of the 20th century, and still others fully ensconced in the 21st century. Simultaneously, human beings are sharing the same planet but seeing the world around us from totally separate experiential frames – even though sometimes all of us are using the same super modern technology.

Change can be merciless, especially to those organisms, structures, and ideas that tether themselves to stationary objects in hopes of preventing change. How many once vaunted institutions and even individuals, have we seen end up like a dry, dead coral reef exposed to the open air and sun by a receding shoreline, the ghost of a once vibrant ecosystem?

When I was a freshman in college I was struggling to keep up, and one of my professors offered her students a speed-reading course. When I was tested, my speed level was at third grade. I felt humiliated but was told I wasn't unusual. In part, she explained, it was because we stop teaching kids "how" to read in third grade and so that is when I stopped *learning* to read and simply *read.* Individuals, marriages, institutions, communities, and even entire nations liter the pages of history as testaments to neglect and resistance to learning instead of open and eager adaptation to the relentless change that is the nature of the cosmos.

When we stop learning and changing, is where we stop.

"Dog is Dog"

Finger Lakes, New York

My dog Rabia, is named after a fifth century Sufi mystic whose name translates from Arabic as, "fourth." She was the fourth daughter in her family and Rabia is my fourth dog. It is not a name that rolls off the tongue and whenever someone asks, inevitably it evokes the questions, "what is it?

Rabia is needy. If you know dogs, and I tell you her mother was a golden and her daddy a lab, then you know she comes by her neediness honestly.

She is also submissive. Not long ago on our early morning walk, we saw a woman heading our way up the sidewalk led by a proud little pug on a leash. As soon as Rabia saw the pug, she got down on her belly, front legs extended with her head on her paws – and wagging her tail. No matter that Rabia was four times that pug's size, she went down and wanted nothing more than to get that little pooch's approval then play.

There is a multitude of recent canine research lauding the intelligence of the species. Dogs, they say, are far more intelligent than humans have recognized – up there with dolphins and whales (and much smarter than cats). Consider, for example, that canines recognized very early in the evolution of the human species that hanging around people was good for their diet. Some of that research suggests the reason dogs make such good guardians, is that they are protecting their meal ticket – humans. Even my submissive mutt turns ferocious when protecting the house. Dogs know what a good thing they've got going and have a multitude of behaviors to evoke our affection, and garner food.

Research also indicates that some dogs can learn hundreds and hundreds of words, amassing a vocabulary that matches a three or four-year-old child. In addition to that, they seem to have an intuition that recognizes human moods with the sensitivity of the most sophisticated radar.

But I remain conflicted about whether or not I wish Rabia could talk.

Those haunting, sorrowful looks she gives me are powerful enough without having words to go with them. I am not at all sure I want to know what she is thinking or feeling because as much as I love my shedding mongrel, she is still a dog.

Some people seem to forget their pet is not human, and minimize the boundaries and differences between humans and other animals. I have great difficulty understanding people with a passionate advocacy for animals when that passion does not extend to advocacy about human injustice and suffering. There is definitely a powerful projection that takes place between humans and their pets, made all the more intense because our pets cannot use words to let us know we have interpreted their expression, motivation, or needs all wrong.

The research I eluded to above, also indicates that for companionship, humans may be better off with dogs that are not quite as smart as the most brilliant of their breed. Moderately intelligent dogs appear to be more responsive to human moods and desires even though less capable in the arena of tricks than the smartest dogs. Dogs may do better with slightly less intelligent human beings too, people like me who don't realize they are being played by their pet.

"Framing Stick Season"
Finger Lakes, New York

We are in the dead of stick season now.

The colors are gone. Vibrancy will not return for at least five months. The charms of Halloween do not even appear in the rearview mirror, and the cozy table of Thanksgiving is a distant sail disappearing over the horizon.

It is not unlike when spring gives winter a hip bump and tries to cut in line early. The shift between those seasons is usually ugly too, with cold rain, sleet, and receding snow revealing nasty liter from poorly socialized dog owners.

Stick season is a darkening gray succession of days enveloping the decaying remains of summer. It will not end until that first big snow of winter.

Our lives have stick seasons too.

There are seasons of life in which we feel like barren shrubs in winter left with naked branches blowing inelegantly in the wind, and once we have entered such gray, it can seem as though green is a color permanently exiled to our past. Those are the moments we have a life-defining decision to make.

My dog is terminally happy. She lives utterly and completely in the moment. If she has ever been sad it was for a few seconds until the next feeling came along and she was totally absorbed by it. She is the very definition of existential, and that is all she is – all in, all the time, in every moment. For good or for ill, and it is both, we are a different kind of creature.

Popular spirituality aside, we cannot *live in the moment*. We can *visit* the moment, but more than that will cause us to become beastly – literally. We have the capacity to remember the past and reflect on it. We have the ability to imagine the future and strategize toward it. In stick season, we need to do both.

In the days when light is dwindling and gray a pall upon the landscape, the ability to remember we have been here before and that we moved through it, can be an enormous benefit. Our ability to will the mind, to refuse the power of the moment to define the rest of life, is a distinctly human blessing.

We get to choose how to frame any moment or event in our lives, rather than remain passively subject to the forces within those circumstances.

When stick season arrives, the one of barren trees or an internal one barren of joy, we have the amazing capacity to frame what we are going through as temporary, and even give it meaning within a greater purpose. Then we have a second blessing, which is to plan how we will make our way into a new season, one that is easier on the eyes and more conducive to growth.

If we find ourselves stuck in stick season, regardless of the time of year, it might be because we are not using the full range of our human capacity. Exercising the powerful gift to frame or re-frame any and all moments, is more than a mental trick. It is the very capacity that allowed us to harness fire, and live in arid deserts, on frozen icecaps, and in danger infested jungles.

"The Seed of Hope"
Finger Lakes, New York

When the small blue flame of love crawls down the candlewick, the last glimmer of light fully within the closing lips of darkness, and despair is as close as the next breath, what keeps hope alive?

When we can imagine edging toward our oldest moment, warmth receding from our fingertips and voices fading from the curvature of our ear forever, what keeps hope alive?

Knowing that Earth, our island home, will one day cease spinning and even the explosive gases of our sun become an unseen mist in frigid space, what keeps hope alive?

Begin with geology, evolutionary biology, and any other light of knowledge we can shine under the blanket in order to see the beginning of life on Earth. Three and three-quarter billion years ago darkness was upon the face of the deep and there was as yet no life. The waters bubbled, swirled, and churned; mire thick with chaos and fever. Then something happened.

In those festering shallows a single cell appeared. Single celled life, bacteria, millions and billions of them. For another *billion* years, until the planet itself was half its current age, life consisted of single cells roiling and broiling and living within the broth of creation wherever water moved, and trickled, and sloshed.

Then two single cells, among all those other single cells cast about in the swill for a billion years, danced together and became one. They sizzled and wriggled and then slithered into two again – two brand new cells! For the first time, two cells had joined and become one, then reproduced into two and so the multiplication continued. Instead of single celled life, it was now multi-celled life hosting unique and varied DNA. Stunning.

In the blink of eternity's eye, a Sequoia tree reached to the clouds like fingers of the Earth grasping for stars. Soon Triceratops rumbled through thick swamps of lush green. Before a light year could dawn, a furless upright animal harnessed fire, crafted tools, and launched the Hubbell telescope. It is an indescribable magnificence compelling awe and wonder.

Seeing this whole thing unfold, on screen through the magic of computer or strolling through the best new high-tech museum of natural history, we gaze upon the incredible four billion year procession of life in all its spectacular diversity, and imbued with mystery and wonder, and we mutter a mildly impressed, *huh.* We witness this unspeakable splendor of the universe exploding and unveiling its wonders before our eyes, and we drive on down the road eating french fries as if it is no big deal.

When we should be trembling and shaking and making uncontrollable noises of amazement and awe, we barely notice. As the Polynesian saying goes, we ride a whale while fishing for minnows.

We dare not ponder it, this astounding microbial birth of life, ignited most likely from elements brought to our planet by fragments of dead stars. To imagine we are actually stardust – that in our bodies we retain the material echo of a long dead star – should set our hair on fire. If we are honest, we cannot fully open our mind to it because it is terrifying: we who are so incredibly small and fragile, are adrift in such a small boat across an ocean of stars.

Alas, amazement and awe are the seeds of hope, requiring nurture and care in order for hope to grow and thrive. Have courage, court awe.

"Forty Thousand Years from Now"
Washington Street, New York

After all the talk, we finally got a peek at a black hole. It isn't the one at the center of our solar system, Sagittarius A, it was in Messier 87 – a nearby galaxy much larger than our own Milky Way.

So, I was a little disappointed that a black hole turns out to look like a glazed red velvet cake donut. I wasn't expecting the silhouette of Darth Vader's helmeted head exactly, but a keyhole would have been nice.

I confess to very little interest in the anniversary of the moon landing. I didn't get patriotic shivers down my spine in 1969, and while I think it is cool there is a moon rock in the stained glass "space window" at the National Cathedral, my only marvel is at the human beings who climb into those space vehicles with a willingness to trust our rudimentary technology. Landing on the moon, or even when we make it as far as mars, amounts to stopping by Seven-Eleven around the block on your way to Mount Kilimanjaro. Sure, it is a beginning, but relative to what there is to explore it does not even amount to a crawl.

Much more compelling, at least to me, is Voyager 1 and 2. After thirty-five years wafting through space on a mission to explore the outer planets of our solar system, the little engines that could are thirteen and fourteen billion miles away, respectively. They left our solar system in 2012 and 2013 and now wander interstellar space, a sensory fingertip for humankind. One of them carries a golden record with human voices and animal sounds from our planet, a note in a bottle for whoever or whatever else is out there.

In case my nonchalance about the moon landing seems hard-hearted or short-sighted, allow me to offer this perspective. Voyager I's new mission, now that it has escaped the heliosphere bubble surrounding our solar system, is an encounter with a star we call AC+79 3888 – a mere 17.6 light years from Earth. That meeting is schedule for forty thousand years from now. No, that is not a typo: forty *thousand* years from now. It seems more likely that Voyager I will fulfill its mission than it does human beings will still be breathing oxygen on Earth by then.

Meanwhile, my dog sits alert in the sunroom staring at squirrels outside. She is content to sit and stare motionless for long periods of time, perhaps imagining herself leaving the limits of the glass bubble enclosing us and jettisoning toward the squirrel who taunts her from the edge of the patio. Her universe does not include AC+ 3888 or Sagittarius A, but her happiness knows no bounds in the world exposed by the length of her leash.

For myself, I am content to enjoy the crisp morning light. The sky is pure blue this morning and the sun, that single star at the center our solar system, washes through the oak and Japanese maples leaving shade art on stunningly green spring grass. We may be able to walk on the moon but where else in the cosmos is there such a lush view as the one I have right here?

Acknowledgements

Miller, Cameron. "My Father Died Last Night" and "Wind on Snow." *Crossroads.* Glenn Lyvers and April Zipser. 1st ed. USA: Inwood Indiana, 2015. 114 and 115. Print.

Miller, Cameron. "Alone Again at the Wok 'N Roll." *Silver Birch Press,* "I Am Waiting Poetry Series." Web. January 24, 2015.

Miller, Cameron. "Behind Closed Eyes." *Festivalforpoetry.com.* Web. May 11, 2018

Miller, Cameron. "Listening to Dark Angels." *Poetry Quarterly.* Glenn Lyvers and April Zipser. Issue 22, Summer 2015. USA: Prolific Press. 8-9. Print.

Miller, Cameron. "Mother Teresa's God." *The Poet's Quest for God.* Oliver Brennan and Todd Swift. Eyewear Press. UK: 2015. 304. Print.

Miller, Cameron. "Loud Angels," "Listening to Time," "Dog is Dog," "When We Stop is Where We Stop," "The End," "Framing Stick Season," "The Seed of Hope," and "Forty Thousand Years from Now," appeared as columns in the series, "Denim Spirit" in *The Finger Lakes Times* (NY).

Miller, Cameron. "Getting Intimate with a Tree," "Rime Ice Around the Heart," "Never Enough," and "Unpacking Wounds" appeared as website posts on *www.subversivepreacher.org.*

In Gratitude

S. Stewart is an extraordinary editor. In addition to refining my awkward efforts, she granted me confidence to publish this book of poems and essays the way birch and chickadees have cheered me through each winter. Thank you, S.

Also, a note of deep gratitude to Ricki, who I only know online through the community of poets but who nudged me from the nest at just the right time. Thank you as well, to Christina, for encouraging me as I left Buffalo to write poems along with fiction, and who took the time to guide me.

Finally, it would seem cold and insensitive of me not to mention my gratitude, often begrudging, to Rabia, my canine companion. She routinely reminds me to look and listen more acutely.

About Cameron Miller

Cameron Miller is a writer and preacher exploring the sacred hiding in plain sight. He writes fiction and poetry, along with essays published weekly in a newspaper column, *Denim Spirit* (Finger Lakes Times – New York). His website is likewise devoted to navigating ordinary spiritual practice: www.subversivepreacher.org.

After thirty-three years of serving Episcopal congregations in Indiana, Ohio, and New York, and a five-year stint simultaneously teaching religion at the college level, Miller left full-time parish ministry in pursuit of his other vocation, writing. While writing was routinely exercised in his ministry through preaching, story-telling, and teaching, the new opportunity to write full-time unleashed previously hidden dimensions of his muse, and eventually, the courage to free the poet within. In addition to writing, he continues to serve part-time in parish ministry, first in Vermont and now the Finger Lakes. Preaching, pastoral care, and the privilege of sharing community with others on a spiritual journey, thins the veil and further reveals the sacred hiding in plain sight.

More from Cameron Miller

"Thoughtwall Café, Espresso in the Third Season of Life," is a novel about the turbulence of mind in the twenties, a decade that mercilessly right-sizes the dreams of childhood, but turns out to be about all stages of life. Unsolicited Press. 2018.

"The Steam Room Diaries," Miller's first novel, is a riotous sequence of stories told by a rotating cadre of strange and lovely characters in a worn-out steam room of an urban Jewish Community Center.

www.subversivepreacher.org is where Miller publishes weekly sermons and reprints of his newspaper column. You can also find subversivepreacher on Facebook and twitter.

About the Press

Unsolicited Press is based in Portland, Oregon. The team produces fiction, nonfiction, and poetry from emerging and award-winning authors.

Learn more at unsolicitedpress.com